**AUTHOR:
MAXWELL STEINBECK**

LABYRINTHS OF TRUTH

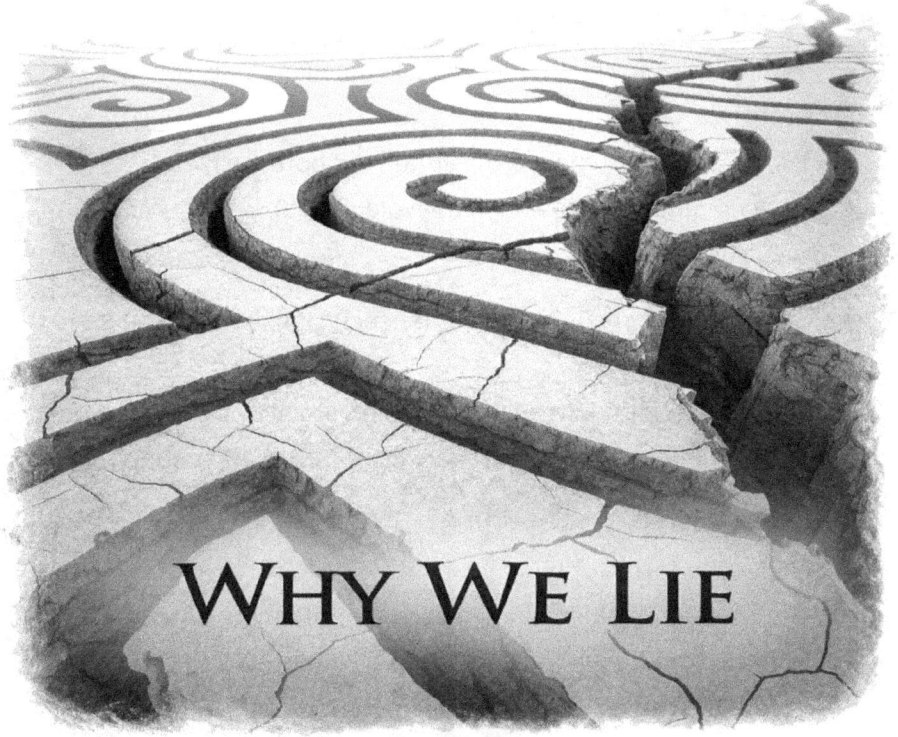

WHY WE LIE

ALL RIGHTS RESERVED.

NO PART OF THIS BOOK MAY BE REPRODUCED WITHOUT
THE WRITTEN PERMISSION OF THE AUTHOR.

PUBLISHING PLATFORM: AMAZON KINDLE DIRECT PUBLISHING

2025

Table of Content

Introduction: What Is a Lie in Today's World? — 3

Chapter 1: Why We Lie — 7

Chapter 2: Types of Lies — 16

Chapter 3: Technological manipulation — 24
- How Digital Systems Shape Belief — 25
- Algorithms, Micro-Targeting, and the Illusion of Choice — 28

Chapter 4: Lies in Relationships — 37
- Types of lies in relationships: from small excuses to betrayals — 38
- Psychological studies of deception for both parties — 41
- How communication can help avoid cheating. — 46

Chapter 5: How to spot a lie — 50
- Strategies for recognizing lies (speech signals, non-verbal signs). — 51
- Tests and techniques that verify the veracity of information. — 56
- Recommendations for the analysis of information sources. — 59

Chapter 6: Ethics and the Future — 65
- Can some forms of lying be justified? — 66
- How can technology change our understanding of truth in the future? — 68
- Potential scenarios of the development of the situation with lies in society. — 71

Conclusion: Is society possible without lies? — 80

INTRODUCTION

What Is a Lie in Today's World?

A lie rarely announces itself. It slips into conversations quietly, hides behind good intentions, and often wears the face of convenience. We tell lies to protect ourselves, to avoid conflict, to preserve an image—or simply because telling the truth feels harder. In a world saturated with information, the boundary between truth and falsehood has never been thinner, nor more dangerous.

At its core, a lie is a deliberate departure from reality. It is the conscious choice to present something false as true. Sometimes it appears harmless—a small distortion meant to spare feelings or smooth social friction. Other times, it grows into something far more consequential, shaping decisions, reputations, markets, and even the fate of nations. From childhood excuses to corporate deceptions and political manipulation, lying is woven into the fabric of human behavior.

Yet lying is not merely a moral failure. It is a psychological strategy.

People lie for many reasons: fear of punishment, desire for acceptance, protection of self-esteem, or the pursuit of power. Psychology views deception as a coping mechanism—an attempt to control outcomes in an uncertain world. Sociology reminds us that cultures silently negotiate which lies are tolerated and which are condemned. What is considered unacceptable in one context may be quietly expected in another.

Lies, in other words, do not exist in a vacuum.

A Brief History of Deception

Humanity has wrestled with truth and falsehood since the beginning of recorded thought. Ancient Greek philosophers understood this struggle well. Plato warned that lies, even when convenient, corrode the moral foundation of society. Aristotle approached deception through ethics and character, asking not only *whether* a lie is wrong, but what kind of person chooses to lie.

During the Middle Ages, lying took on religious weight. In Christian doctrine, falsehood was considered a sin—an offense not just against others, but against divine order itself. And yet, even then, exceptions quietly emerged. Lies were sometimes justified in the name of faith, loyalty, or protection of the innocent. The moral tension never disappeared; it merely changed shape.

History shows us that while attitudes toward lying evolve, the practice itself remains constant.

Lies in the Modern World

Today, deception has found a powerful ally: technology.

The digital age has transformed how information is created, shared, and consumed. News no longer passes exclusively through editors, institutions, or ethical filters. Anyone with an internet connection can become a source. This democratization of information has undeniable benefits—but it has also opened the floodgates to misinformation, manipulation, and deliberate falsehoods on an unprecedented scale.

Social media platforms reward attention, not accuracy. Algorithms amplify content that provokes emotion—fear, outrage, confirmation—regardless of whether it is true. A sensational lie often travels faster than a careful fact. Over time, distorted narratives begin to feel familiar, and familiarity is easily mistaken for truth.

One of the most striking examples of modern deception is the Cambridge Analytica scandal, where personal data was weaponized to influence political behavior. It revealed not only how lies spread, but how precisely they can be targeted—custom-designed for individual fears, biases, and beliefs.

Why We Lie

Despite its consequences, lying persists because it works—at least in the short term.

People lie to avoid punishment, to maintain control, to construct a more desirable version of themselves. A student lies to escape embarrassment. A professional exaggerates achievements to gain advantage. A corporation reshapes facts to protect profit. In some cases, lies are even framed as kindness—meant to shield others from pain.

Research in psychology suggests that deception is not always selfish. So-called "altruistic lies" are told to protect relationships or spare emotional harm. The uncomfortable truth is that many lies succeed precisely because they feel justified.

But success comes at a cost.

Every lie subtly reshapes reality. Over time, repeated falsehoods distort perception, erode trust, and weaken the shared framework that allows societies to function. In the digital age, where lies scale instantly and globally, this cost is no longer personal—it is collective.

Understanding why we lie is the first step toward resisting deception—both from others and from ourselves. As misinformation becomes more sophisticated, critical thinking and ethical responsibility are no longer optional skills. They are tools for survival.

CHAPTER 1

Why We Lie

Lying is rarely the result of cruelty alone. More often, it is born from fear, pressure, and the instinct to survive—socially, emotionally, or professionally. While honesty is celebrated as a moral ideal, deception remains a practical tool many people reach for when truth feels too costly. To understand why lying is so deeply embedded in human behavior, we must first examine the psychological forces that make it feel necessary.

Fear as the First Catalyst

Fear is one of the most powerful motivators behind deception. It operates quietly, often beneath conscious awareness, shaping decisions long before moral reasoning has a chance to intervene. Fear of punishment, fear of rejection, fear of humiliation, fear of loss—each can push an otherwise honest person toward a lie.

Consider a simple childhood example: a student breaks a window at school. Faced with the certainty of punishment and disappointment, the child claims it was an accident or blames an unseen cause. In this moment, lying functions as a psychological shield. The truth threatens immediate consequences; the lie offers a chance—however fragile—of escape.

This mechanism does not disappear with age. It matures.

In professional environments, fear often takes subtler forms. An employee who underperforms on a project may exaggerate results or shift responsibility onto a colleague. Not because deception feels right, but because the perceived cost of honesty—loss of status, income, or security—feels unbearable. In such cases, lying becomes a risk calculation rather than a moral choice.

Psychological research consistently shows that when individuals feel trapped, cornered, or evaluated under high stakes, their likelihood of deception increases. The brain, prioritizing survival, often treats social threats with the same urgency as physical ones. Reputation, after all, can determine access to opportunity, belonging, and safety.

Pressure and the Weight of Expectation

Fear rarely acts alone. It is reinforced by pressure—explicit or implicit—exerted by institutions, families, peers, and culture itself.

From a young age, individuals learn that approval is conditional. Good grades, good behavior, success, attractiveness, productivity—each becomes a silent requirement. When expectations exceed personal capacity, deception emerges as a coping strategy.

Take the example of students competing for scholarships. Faced with intense academic pressure and limited opportunities, some manipulate grades, embellish achievements, or omit failures. The lie is not driven by greed alone, but by the terror of falling behind in a system that equates worth with performance.

In adulthood, this pressure only intensifies.

Workplaces often reward outcomes rather than processes, results rather than honesty. Employees learn quickly which truths are welcome—and which are not. A culture that punishes failure but praises confidence quietly incentivizes deception. In such environments, honesty becomes risky, while selective truth-telling becomes strategic.

Digital culture magnifies this dynamic. Social media platforms transform everyday life into a performance, encouraging users to curate an image of success, happiness, and fulfillment. Vacations are exaggerated, achievements inflated, struggles hidden. The lie here is rarely spoken outright; it is implied through omission and presentation. Yet its psychological effect is real—both for the person constructing the illusion and for those consuming it.

The pressure to appear "successful" does not merely distort reality; it reshapes identity.

Avoiding Consequences: The Logic of Short-Term Survival

Beyond fear and pressure lies a third driver of deception: the desire to avoid consequences. This is perhaps the most rational form of lying—and the most dangerous.

In business, the temptation to delay bad news or misrepresent financial realities is well-documented. When companies face declining profits or internal failures, executives may withhold information, manipulate data, or frame losses as temporary setbacks. The goal is rarely long-term deception; it is time—time to fix the problem, time to protect investors, time to preserve reputation.

Yet history shows that such lies compound rather than dissolve risk.

The same logic applies in legal and personal contexts. Individuals facing legal trouble may deny wrongdoing despite overwhelming evidence, hoping to escape accountability. While this may offer temporary relief, it often escalates consequences, transforming manageable problems into irreversible crises.

Psychologically, this behavior reflects a common bias: humans tend to prioritize immediate relief over long-term stability. A lie reduces anxiety in the moment, even if it increases danger later. The brain rewards short-term escape, not long-term integrity.

When Lying Becomes a Habit

What begins as a defensive response can gradually harden into habit. Repeated deception reshapes internal narratives, making dishonesty feel normal—even necessary. Over time, individuals may stop experiencing guilt altogether, replacing moral discomfort with justification.

This is how personal lies scale into systemic ones.

Organizations normalize misinformation. Political movements rationalize manipulation. Societies grow tolerant of distortion, as long as it aligns with identity or belief. The line between truth and convenience blurs, and eventually, truth itself becomes negotiable.

Understanding these psychological foundations is not about excusing deception. It is about recognizing its roots. Only by acknowledging fear, pressure, and consequence-avoidance as core drivers can individuals—and societies—begin to address the conditions that make lying feel inevitable.

Social Forces Behind Deception

Group Pressure, Norms, and Collective Blindness

If fear explains why individuals lie, society explains why lies spread. Deception does not remain a private act for long. It is shaped, amplified, and often rewarded by group dynamics. Humans are social beings, and our need to belong can quietly override our commitment to truth.

From early childhood, conformity is reinforced. Children learn which answers are praised and which are punished, which emotions are acceptable and which must be hidden. By adulthood, this conditioning is deeply internalized. People do not merely fear being wrong—they fear being excluded.

Group pressure rarely demands direct dishonesty. Instead, it creates an environment where silence, omission, or selective truth become the safest options. When everyone appears to agree, dissent feels dangerous. Speaking the truth begins to look like betrayal rather than integrity.

This phenomenon has been widely studied in psychology. Classic experiments on conformity demonstrated that individuals will knowingly agree with false statements if they believe the group expects it. The discomfort of social isolation often outweighs the discomfort of lying—to others and to oneself.

The Comfort of Shared Illusions

One of the most powerful social drivers of deception is the shared illusion. When many people participate in the same distortion, it begins to feel real. The lie gains legitimacy through repetition and consensus.

Workplace cultures offer a clear example. In organizations where unrealistic optimism is encouraged, employees quickly learn to avoid bad news. Problems are minimized, warnings softened, risks reframed. Over time, everyone participates in maintaining the illusion that "everything is under control." No single lie feels decisive—but together, they create systemic blindness.

The cost of breaking this illusion is often high. Whistleblowers frequently face isolation, retaliation, or dismissal. As a result, many choose silence. The lie survives not because it is convincing, but because telling the truth feels unsafe.

Innocent Lies and Their Hidden Weight

Not all deception is dramatic. Much of it appears harmless, even kind.

So-called "white lies" are woven into daily life: polite compliments, softened opinions, emotional buffering. A friend asks for honesty but hopes for reassurance. A colleague seeks feedback but expects encouragement. These small distortions help maintain social harmony and avoid conflict.

Yet even innocent lies carry weight.

When repeated, they blur emotional boundaries and weaken trust. Relationships built on constant emotional editing lose depth. People begin to wonder which words are real and which are strategic. The absence of conflict may feel peaceful, but it often conceals distance.

In intimate relationships, small deceptions accumulate quietly. Habits are hidden, disappointments unspoken, desires suppressed. When the truth eventually surfaces—as it often does—the damage feels disproportionate to the lie itself. What hurts is not the fact, but the realization that authenticity was replaced by performance.

Deception at Scale: Politics and Power

When deception moves from personal relationships into systems of power, its consequences expand dramatically.

Political environments are especially vulnerable. Leaders operate under immense pressure to appear competent, decisive, and victorious. Admitting uncertainty or failure can be interpreted as weakness. In such climates, distortion becomes tempting.

Modern political communication often relies on emotional narratives rather than factual complexity. Simplified messages spread faster. Fear mobilizes more effectively than nuance. As a result, selective truths, exaggerations, and omissions become standard tools.

The danger lies not in a single false claim, but in the normalization of manipulation. When citizens expect dishonesty, trust erodes. Cynicism replaces engagement. People stop asking whether information is true and begin asking whether it serves their side.

At this stage, deception becomes self-sustaining.

Corporate Lies and the Logic of Profit

Business history offers equally sobering lessons. Corporate deception rarely begins with malice. It often starts with pressure to perform, compete, and grow.

Companies that manipulate data, hide risks, or mislead consumers usually justify their actions as temporary measures. The goal is survival, market confidence, or shareholder reassurance. Yet once deception enters decision-making processes, it reshapes organizational culture.

The collapse of major corporations due to accounting fraud, false advertising, or environmental cover-ups illustrates how systemic lies destroy not only trust but entire institutions. Employees lose jobs, investors lose savings, communities suffer consequences—all rooted in decisions made to avoid short-term discomfort.

In these cases, the lie is not just told—it is engineered, maintained, and defended.

Technology and the Acceleration of Falsehood

Digital platforms have transformed the scale and speed of deception. Information now travels faster than verification. Algorithms reward engagement, not accuracy. Content that provokes outrage or affirmation spreads more efficiently than careful analysis.

This environment amplifies existing biases. People are more likely to encounter information that confirms their beliefs, reinforcing confidence even when the foundation is false. The result is fragmentation—multiple versions of reality coexisting without dialogue.

Importantly, most participants in this system do not see themselves as liars. They share information they believe is true or emotionally satisfying. Intent becomes secondary to impact. Misinformation spreads not because people wish to deceive, but because systems are designed to reward attention over truth.

Ethical Responsibility in a Deceptive World

Understanding the social roots of lying forces a difficult question: where does responsibility lie?

It is easy to blame individuals. Harder to confront cultures that reward distortion, punish honesty, and equate success with appearance. Ethics cannot survive on personal virtue alone. They require environments where truth is protected, not penalized.

Media literacy, critical thinking, and institutional transparency are not luxuries—they are defenses. Without them, societies drift toward convenient narratives and away from reality.

Yet responsibility also remains personal. Each lie—small or large—contributes to a broader climate. Each moment of honesty, especially when uncomfortable, resists that drift.

Choosing Truth in an Uncomfortable World

Lying persists not because humans are inherently immoral, but because truth is often inconvenient. It demands courage, patience, and tolerance for uncertainty. Deception offers speed and safety—at a cost.

If we wish to navigate the labyrinth of truth, we must first acknowledge its walls. Only then can we begin to choose honesty—not as a moral slogan, but as a deliberate, often difficult act.

CHAPTER 2

Types of Lies

Innocent Lies and the Quiet Architecture of Deception

Not all lies announce themselves as threats. Some arrive gently, wrapped in politeness, care, or social courtesy. They are the lies we tell to smooth conversations, protect feelings, and avoid discomfort. Often dismissed as harmless, these "innocent" or mitigating lies form the most common—and most underestimated—category of deception.

In everyday life, such lies are everywhere. A compliment offered without conviction. A reassurance that conceals doubt. A silence that replaces an inconvenient truth. These moments rarely feel unethical. On the contrary, they are often rewarded. Social life depends on them.

When someone asks whether their new outfit looks good, the expected answer is rarely an honest critique. The socially acceptable response is encouragement. The goal is not accuracy, but harmony. In this context, truth becomes secondary to emotional comfort.

Research in social psychology consistently shows that most people prefer minor dishonesty to interpersonal tension. Avoiding embarrassment, disappointment, or conflict feels more urgent than factual precision. These lies are rarely told with malicious intent. They are acts of social lubrication.

Yet their impact should not be underestimated.

Why We Tell "White Lies"

Innocent lies are rooted in deeply human motivations. At their core lies the desire for acceptance. Humans evolved in small groups where belonging meant survival. Open conflict carried risks. Harmony ensured protection.

That instinct remains active today. Many people instinctively soften reality to preserve relationships. The lie becomes a shield—protecting both the speaker and the listener from discomfort.

Parents frequently use such lies with children. Difficult truths are postponed or simplified. A grandparent's absence is explained away. A painful reality is delayed until the child is "old enough to understand." These choices are often made out of care, not deceit.

In romantic relationships, innocent lies often function as emotional buffers. A partner says, "I'm just tired," when something deeper is wrong. The truth is postponed in the name of peace. Over time, however, postponed truths tend to accumulate.

In professional environments, mitigating lies are even more normalized. Performance is "improving." Results are "promising." Setbacks are "temporary." Language becomes a tool for reassurance rather than clarity. While this can motivate teams in the short term, it often obscures problems that require attention.

What begins as encouragement can quietly drift into distortion.

The Emotional Cost of Harmless Deception

Although innocent lies feel safe, they subtly reshape relationships. When truth is consistently softened, authenticity suffers. Conversations become performances. Emotional distance grows behind polite words.

Trust does not collapse suddenly. It erodes gradually.

A relationship built on constant emotional editing lacks resilience. When honesty finally emerges—often during moments of crisis—it feels shocking, even if the lie itself was small. The sense of betrayal comes not from the fact that the truth was hidden, but from how long it was postponed.

This pattern appears frequently in long-term partnerships. Small omissions, repeated over time, create parallel realities. When these realities collide, the damage is often disproportionate to the original lie.

In workplaces, the consequences can be systemic. Employees accustomed to "positive framing" may stop reporting risks. Leaders receive filtered information. Decision-making becomes detached from reality. Eventually, the cost of politeness exceeds the cost of honesty.

Social Media and the Polished Self

Technology has dramatically expanded the space for innocent deception. Social media platforms reward presentation over truth. Users curate their lives, highlighting success and hiding struggle.

This behavior is rarely perceived as lying. It is described as "sharing selectively." Yet the cumulative effect is powerful. When millions of people present idealized versions of themselves, comparison becomes distorted. Reality feels insufficient.

The pressure to appear happy, successful, and fulfilled encourages subtle dishonesty—not just toward others, but toward oneself. People begin to believe the image they project. The gap between lived experience and public identity widens.

In this environment, innocent lies are no longer isolated. They form a collective illusion. Everyone knows the image is incomplete, yet everyone participates. The lie becomes normalized.

When Innocent Lies Become a Gateway

The most important danger of mitigating lies is not their immediate effect, but their trajectory.

When deception becomes acceptable in small matters, ethical boundaries shift. The question is no longer "Is this true?" but "Is this useful?" Once that shift occurs, escalation becomes easier.

In business, this progression is well documented. Companies often begin with optimistic language. Over time, optimism shades into exaggeration. Exaggeration becomes misrepresentation. Eventually, data is manipulated to sustain the narrative.

The same pattern appears in politics. Early image management gives way to selective disclosure. Selective disclosure turns into disinformation. The original justification

From Politeness to Power: When Lies Become Tools

Once deception proves useful in small matters, it rarely stays small. What begins as emotional protection can evolve into a strategy. In politics and business, lies are rarely spontaneous. They are designed, tested, refined, and deployed with precision.

Unlike innocent lies, manipulative deception is intentional and strategic. Its purpose is not harmony, but control.

Political manipulation offers some of the clearest examples. Leaders operate in an environment where perception often outweighs reality. Public support depends not only on actions, but on narratives. In this context, truth becomes negotiable.

Political lies are rarely direct. Instead, they rely on framing. Facts are not invented; they are arranged. Certain details are amplified, others buried. The result is a version of reality that feels coherent while remaining incomplete.

Modern political campaigns often focus less on informing voters and more on shaping emotional responses. Fear, pride, resentment, and hope are powerful motivators. When facts do not produce the desired emotion, narratives are adjusted accordingly.

One of the most effective techniques is simplification. Complex problems are reduced to clear villains and easy solutions. Nuance disappears. The lie succeeds not because it is elaborate, but because it is easy to understand.

Corporate Deception and the Language of Trust

In the corporate world, deception often hides behind professionalism. Financial reports, marketing language, and public statements are crafted to inspire confidence. As long as the company appears stable, few questions are asked.

Corporate lies often emerge gradually. Early warnings are softened. Risks are reframed as opportunities. Losses become "temporary setbacks." Over time, the internal culture adapts. Employees learn which truths are welcome and which are not.

This environment discourages honesty. Those who speak plainly are labeled pessimistic or disloyal. Silence becomes safer than truth. Eventually, decision-makers operate within an echo chamber of reassuring half-truths.

History offers many examples of this progression. Major corporate scandals rarely begin with criminal intent. They begin with small compromises—numbers adjusted, projections overstated, uncomfortable facts delayed. Each step feels manageable. Each step makes the next easier.

When the truth finally surfaces, the damage is amplified by duration. The lie did not merely exist; it was maintained.

Psychological Tricks That Make Lies Work

Manipulation succeeds not because people are foolish, but because human psychology is predictable. The most effective lies exploit natural cognitive tendencies.

One of the most powerful mechanisms is **confirmation bias**. People instinctively seek information that supports their existing beliefs. When a lie aligns with what someone already thinks or fears, it feels true.

This bias explains why misinformation spreads rapidly in polarized environments. Competing groups consume entirely different versions of reality. Each side feels informed. Each side feels justified.

Another common mechanism is **emotional priming**. When information is delivered in a state of heightened emotion—fear, anger, pride—critical thinking weakens. The brain prioritizes response over analysis.

Manipulators understand this well. Messages are crafted to provoke emotion first and explanation second. By the time facts are questioned, the emotional reaction has already taken hold.

There is also **cognitive dissonance**, the discomfort we feel when actions conflict with beliefs. To reduce this discomfort, people often adjust their interpretation of reality rather than their behavior. Lies become self-protective narratives.

This is why people may defend false information even after it has been disproven. Admitting the truth would require admitting error, vulnerability, or responsibility. The lie feels safer.

The Illusion of Choice in the Information Age

Technology has not created deception, but it has accelerated it. Algorithms reward engagement, not accuracy. Content that provokes strong reactions spreads faster than content that informs.

Social platforms personalize information streams. Over time, users encounter fewer opposing views. This creates informational bubbles—closed systems where certain narratives are continuously reinforced.

Within these spaces, lies do not feel like lies. They feel like common knowledge.

The illusion of choice deepens the problem. People believe they are independently informed, unaware of how content is filtered. This perceived autonomy strengthens confidence in false conclusions.

As a result, manipulation no longer feels imposed. It feels self-directed.

When Deception Becomes Normal

The greatest danger is not that lies exist, but that they become expected. When deception is assumed, trust collapses. Institutions lose credibility. Relationships become transactional.

In such environments, honesty feels risky. Speaking truth becomes an act of defiance rather than responsibility.

Yet history shows that societies built on sustained deception become fragile. Decisions based on false premises eventually fail. Reality reasserts itself, often harshly.

Choosing Awareness Over Illusion

Understanding the types of lies—innocent, strategic, psychological—does not make us immune to them. But it gives us distance. Awareness slows reaction. It creates space for questioning.

The path out of deception is not absolute honesty at all times, but conscious honesty. It is the willingness to ask: *Why is this being said? Who benefits? What is missing?*

Truth is rarely comfortable. But it is stable.

As we move deeper into the labyrinth of modern information, the ability to recognize manipulation becomes a form of literacy. Not intellectual superiority, but survival skill.

The lies around us will not disappear. But neither will our capacity to see through them—if we choose to use it.

CHAPTER 3

Technological manipulation

How Digital Systems Shape Belief

The architecture of deception in the digital age

Social networks were once imagined as tools of connection—digital bridges linking people across borders, cultures, and ideas. In practice, they have become something more complex and far more powerful: systems that quietly shape perception, amplify emotion, and, at times, distort reality itself. In this environment, misinformation does not spread accidentally. It moves with structure, speed, and intent.

The defining feature of modern social platforms is not simply communication, but **velocity**. Information travels faster than reflection. Content is shared long before it is questioned. Unlike traditional media, where editors acted as gatekeepers, social networks place the responsibility of verification on the individual—often at moments when emotion overrides judgment.

This shift has profound consequences. False information, especially when framed to provoke fear, outrage, or moral superiority, often spreads faster than verified facts. Studies conducted after the 2016 U.S. presidential election demonstrated that fake news stories consistently generated more engagement—likes, shares, comments—than accurate reporting. The reason is not mystery; it is psychology. Humans are wired to react to emotionally charged narratives, and social platforms are designed to reward precisely that reaction.

Why misinformation thrives online

One of the most dangerous aspects of misinformation is how ordinary it appears. Fake news rarely announces itself as false. It adopts the visual language of legitimacy—headlines, images, authoritative tone—while bypassing the standards that once governed public information.

Social networks enable this by allowing users to share content instantly, often without reading beyond a headline. In this environment, repetition replaces evidence. When people encounter the same claim multiple times, even from unreliable sources, the mind begins to treat familiarity as truth. Psychologists refer to this phenomenon as the **illusory truth effect**: repeated statements feel more credible, regardless of their accuracy.

A striking example of this dynamic was a fabricated story about a panda allegedly escaping from a zoo and roaming a city as a "heroic figure," rescuing people from disasters. Absurd as it was, the story accumulated millions of shares. Its success revealed a troubling reality: plausibility matters less than emotional appeal. In the economy of attention, entertainment often outperforms truth.

The role of algorithms: invisible editors of reality

At the center of this ecosystem sit algorithms—complex systems designed to personalize content and maximize engagement. These algorithms decide what users see, how often they see it, and in what emotional context it appears. While presented as neutral tools, they are anything but.

Algorithms learn from behavior. Every click, pause, share, or reaction teaches the system what holds attention. Over time, this creates a feedback loop: users are shown more of what they already respond to, while contradictory perspectives gradually disappear. The result is the formation of **information echo chambers**, where beliefs are reinforced rather than challenged.

Inside these echo chambers, misinformation thrives. Content that aligns with existing views is accepted with little scrutiny, while opposing information is dismissed as biased or hostile. This is not accidental—it mirrors a well-documented cognitive bias known as

confirmation bias, the human tendency to seek out and trust information that supports preexisting beliefs.

Algorithms do not create this bias, but they amplify it at scale.

Emotional amplification as a business model

Social platforms are not designed primarily to inform; they are designed to retain attention. Emotionally charged content—fear, anger, moral outrage—keeps users engaged longer. As a result, algorithms tend to prioritize content that triggers strong reactions, regardless of its factual accuracy.

During major political events, this mechanism becomes especially visible. In multiple countries, including the United States, Brazil, and India, election periods have coincided with surges in misinformation. False narratives spread rapidly, not because they are persuasive in a rational sense, but because they provoke emotional alignment: "us versus them," "threat versus safety," "truth versus corruption."

In such contexts, misinformation does more than misinform—it polarizes. Society fractures into opposing camps, each consuming a different version of reality. Dialogue becomes impossible when there is no shared factual ground.

Deepfakes and the erosion of visual truth

If fake news undermines trust in words, **deepfake technology** threatens trust in sight itself. Advances in artificial intelligence now allow the creation of highly realistic videos in which individuals appear to say or do things that never occurred. The implications are profound.

In 2018, manipulated videos surfaced that convincingly altered the speech of public figures. Although these examples were later exposed, they demonstrated how easily visual evidence—once considered the strongest form of proof—can be fabricated. As deepfakes become more accessible, the line between reality and fabrication grows increasingly fragile.

The danger lies not only in deception, but in doubt. When people can no longer trust what they see, skepticism spreads indiscriminately. Genuine evidence is dismissed alongside falsehoods. This phenomenon, sometimes described as **epistemic erosion**, weakens society's ability to agree on basic facts.

Psychological consequences of constant misinformation

The impact of digital manipulation extends beyond politics and public discourse. Continuous exposure to misinformation—especially content framed around danger, betrayal, or catastrophe—has measurable effects on mental health. Research links excessive consumption of alarming or deceptive content to increased anxiety, stress, and emotional exhaustion.

In this state, critical thinking declines. When individuals feel overwhelmed, they are more likely to rely on emotional shortcuts rather than analysis. Ironically, anxiety itself becomes a tool of manipulation, pushing people to share information impulsively in an attempt to regain control or warn others.

Young people are particularly vulnerable. Growing up in a digital environment where information flows continuously, many lack the cognitive frameworks needed to distinguish credible sources from fabricated ones. Without deliberate education in media literacy, the digital world becomes a landscape where appearance substitutes for truth.

Algorithms, Micro-Targeting, and the Illusion of Choice

Algorithms as silent persuaders

Algorithms are often described as neutral tools—mathematical systems designed to optimize user experience. In reality, they function as silent persuaders, shaping not only what people see but how they interpret the world. Their influence is subtle, continuous, and largely invisible to those affected by it.

Every interaction on a digital platform becomes data. Likes, comments, viewing time, scrolling speed—all of it is recorded, analyzed, and translated into predictions about future behavior. Over time, platforms do not simply respond to user preferences; they begin to anticipate and guide them. What feels like personal choice is often the result of curated exposure.

This creates a powerful asymmetry. Users believe they are freely navigating information, while platforms quietly determine which narratives gain prominence and which fade into obscurity. The danger lies not in overt censorship, but in selective visibility—the gradual narrowing of what feels real, relevant, or possible.

The rise of micro-targeted persuasion

One of the most consequential developments in digital manipulation is micro-targeting. Unlike traditional mass messaging, micro-targeting allows tailored content to be delivered to specific individuals or groups based on psychological profiles, behavioral patterns, and emotional vulnerabilities.

Political campaigns, corporations, and interest groups can now deliver different versions of reality to different audiences—often simultaneously. A message designed to evoke fear may be shown to one group, while another group receives reassurance or moral validation. These audiences rarely see each other's messages, making manipulation difficult to detect and nearly impossible to challenge publicly.

This strategy was widely documented during several recent election cycles. In Brazil's 2018 presidential election, social media became the dominant channel for political communication. False narratives, distributed through encrypted messaging platforms and amplified by algorithms, shaped voter perceptions at scale. Similar patterns emerged in India, Eastern Europe, and parts of Africa, where digital campaigns exploited social divisions with remarkable efficiency.

What makes micro-targeting especially dangerous is its psychological precision. Messages are not designed to persuade rationally; they are designed to resonate emotionally. Fear, resentment, pride, and identity become tools—not arguments.

Confirmation bias at industrial scale

Human cognition has always been vulnerable to bias. What has changed is scale. Algorithms now amplify confirmation bias across millions of users simultaneously, transforming a natural cognitive tendency into a structural feature of digital life.

When individuals are repeatedly exposed to content that aligns with their beliefs, dissenting information begins to feel not merely incorrect, but hostile. This hardens opinions and reduces openness to dialogue. Over time, disagreement becomes moralized: those who think differently are no longer mistaken—they are dangerous, corrupt, or malicious.

This dynamic explains why misinformation is so resilient. Correcting false claims often fails not because evidence is weak, but because it threatens identity. In algorithmically curated environments, belief becomes part of self-definition. To question information is to question belonging.

The illusion of popularity and manufactured consensus

Another powerful mechanism of manipulation is the illusion of consensus. When content appears popular—trending topics, viral posts, high engagement—it gains credibility by association. Humans instinctively interpret popularity as a signal of truth or importance.

Algorithms reinforce this tendency by promoting content that already performs well. As engagement grows, visibility increases, creating a self-reinforcing loop. Fake news often exploits this dynamic by generating early bursts of activity—sometimes through coordinated networks of bots or paid accounts—giving false narratives the appearance of widespread acceptance.

A well-known case involved viral claims about miracle medical products and conspiracy-driven health advice. Despite lacking scientific support, such content gained traction through algorithmic amplification, leading many to distrust established medical guidance. In some instances, the consequences were not merely intellectual, but physical.

Corporate incentives and ethical blind spots

At the core of technological manipulation lies a fundamental tension: platforms profit from engagement, not accuracy. While most technology companies publicly acknowledge the problem of misinformation, their economic models often reward the very dynamics that sustain it.

Emotionally charged content keeps users scrolling. Polarizing narratives increase interaction. Outrage sustains attention. In this context, misinformation is not an anomaly—it is a byproduct of incentive structures.

This raises difficult ethical questions. To what extent should platforms be responsible for the societal effects of their systems? Are they neutral hosts, or active participants in shaping public consciousness? While some argue that responsibility lies with users to verify information, this view ignores the power imbalance between individuals and algorithmic systems designed by teams of behavioral scientists and engineers.

Data, surveillance, and behavioral prediction

Modern algorithms rely on unprecedented levels of personal data. Social networks track not only explicit actions, but inferred traits—political leanings, emotional states, personality characteristics. This data enables increasingly accurate predictions about behavior and susceptibility to persuasion.

In effect, users become both consumers and products. Their attention is sold, their behavior optimized, their beliefs influenced—often without explicit consent or awareness. The manipulation is rarely coercive; it is frictionless, operating through convenience and personalization.

Over time, this erodes autonomy. When choices are continuously shaped by unseen forces, the boundary between influence and control becomes blurred.

Awareness as the first defense

Understanding algorithmic manipulation does not require technical expertise, but it does require intellectual humility. Recognizing that our perceptions are shaped—sometimes deliberately—opens the door to critical engagement.

The most important skill in the digital age is not skepticism alone, but meta-awareness: the ability to question not only information, but the systems that deliver it. Why am I seeing this content? Who benefits from my reaction? What perspectives are missing?

Without this awareness, individuals remain vulnerable to narratives crafted not to inform, but to direct behavior.

Case studies: the impact of fake news on public opinion

Fake news is not merely inaccurate information. In the digital age, it has evolved into a strategic instrument capable of shaping beliefs, directing behavior, and altering the course of political and social events. Its power lies not in isolated falsehoods, but in systematic repetition, emotional framing, and algorithmic amplification.

One of the most widely cited examples remains the 2016 United States presidential election. During the campaign, a series of fabricated stories circulated widely across social media platforms. Among the most infamous was the claim that Democratic candidate Hillary Clinton was involved in a child-trafficking operation allegedly run from a Washington, D.C. pizzeria. Although the story was entirely fictitious and repeatedly debunked, it gained enormous traction online.

The significance of this case lies not in the absurdity of the claim, but in its psychological effectiveness. For individuals already distrustful of political elites, the narrative aligned with pre-existing suspicions. Research later showed that people exposed to politically congruent fake news were significantly more likely to accept it as true. This reflects a well-documented cognitive mechanism: confirmation bias, the tendency to favor information that supports existing beliefs while dismissing contradictory evidence.

Emotion as the engine of virality

Emotion plays a central role in the spread of fake news. Content that evokes fear, anger, or moral outrage is far more likely to be shared than neutral or factual reporting. In fast-moving digital environments, users rarely pause to verify claims; they react.

This dynamic creates fertile ground for manipulation. When emotionally charged narratives dominate information feeds, rational evaluation gives way to instinctive response. The result is not simply misinformation, but emotional conditioning, where repeated exposure shapes attitudes and expectations over time.

During periods of crisis—elections, pandemics, military conflicts—this effect intensifies. False reports can escalate tensions, undermine trust in institutions, and provoke real-world consequences. In several documented cases, viral misinformation has contributed to public panic, harassment campaigns, and even acts of violence.

Polarization and the erosion of shared reality

Beyond individual belief, fake news reshapes society by deepening polarization. As algorithmic systems reinforce ideological bubbles, communities increasingly inhabit separate informational worlds. Media outlets, once perceived as neutral intermediaries, become labeled as partisan or hostile depending on audience alignment.

This fragmentation erodes the possibility of constructive dialogue. When groups cannot agree on basic facts, disagreement shifts from policy to identity. The question is no longer *what is true*, but *who are you with*. Such conditions are fundamentally incompatible with democratic deliberation, which depends on shared reference points and mutual recognition.

Over time, this dynamic undermines social cohesion. Trust declines—not only in media, but in institutions, experts, and even fellow citizens.

Technology as an amplifier, not a cause

It is important to recognize that technology does not invent deception; it amplifies it. Lies have always existed, but digital systems have removed traditional barriers: editorial oversight, time for reflection, and accountability. What once spread slowly now travels instantly, crossing borders and languages with ease.

Social platforms such as Facebook, X (formerly Twitter), and Instagram play a central role in this transformation. Their recommendation systems, optimized for engagement, inadvertently reward sensationalism. Users are shown more of what captures attention, not what reflects reality.

When misinformation enters these systems, it is not merely tolerated—it is often structurally advantaged.

Countering misinformation: limits and possibilities

How can societies respond to the influence of fake news? There is no single solution, but several approaches offer meaningful resistance.

First, education remains the most effective long-term strategy. Media literacy—teaching individuals how to evaluate sources, recognize manipulation, and understand cognitive biases—reduces susceptibility to false narratives. Studies suggest that even brief interventions can significantly improve critical evaluation skills.

Second, platforms bear responsibility. While complete neutrality is unrealistic, transparency is achievable. Labeling disputed content, reducing algorithmic amplification of demonstrably false claims, and supporting independent fact-checking initiatives can limit harm without resorting to censorship.

Third, individual behavior matters. Users who pause before sharing, consult multiple sources, and engage respectfully with opposing views contribute to healthier information ecosystems. Small shifts in collective behavior can produce meaningful change.

A shared responsibility

Fake news is not merely a technological problem; it is a social one. It thrives where trust is low, emotions run high, and critical thinking is neglected. Addressing it requires cooperation among educators, technologists, policymakers, and citizens.

The challenge of misinformation forces a deeper question: **What kind of information culture do we want to inhabit?** One driven by outrage and immediacy, or one grounded in reflection and responsibility?

Reclaiming agency in a manipulated world

Technological manipulation does not eliminate free will, but it constrains it. Algorithms shape what we see, hear, and consider—but awareness restores agency. By understanding how digital systems influence perception, individuals can reclaim the capacity to choose deliberately rather than reactively.

In an age of information overload, truth does not disappear quietly—it must be defended consciously. The task of our time is not to eliminate deception entirely, but to recognize it, resist it, and refuse to become passive participants in its spread.

Only then can technology serve human judgment, rather than replace it.

CHAPTER 4

Lies in Relationships

Types of lies in relationships: from small excuses to betrayals

Lying in a relationship can range from minor excuses to serious betrayals. It touches the greatest aspects of trust between people and can have both innocent motives and devastating consequences. Understanding the nature of lies in relationships will help not only by analyzing specific situations, but also by understanding how and why people choose to lie, even in the most intimate relationships.

Lies often start with small excuses that people make to avoid conflict or to stay within their comfort zone. Let's imagine a situation where one of the partners says they have to work late but actually spends time with friends at a bar. Perhaps he does not want to confront his partner or is afraid of jealousy, so he makes up excuses. From the liar's perspective, it seems like an innocent ruse that protects both of them from unnecessary stress. However, even such small deceptions can lead to serious problems.

The psychology behind such excuses is related to the desire to avoid conflict and discomfort. People who seek harmony in relationships sometimes choose deception as a way to maintain temporary stability. They may believe that being honest will cause a strong reaction from their partner or hurt their feelings. This phenomenon is often called a 'white lie,' and it appears harmless at first glance.

However, there is another level of deception – lies on a larger scale that can destroy trust in a relationship. This includes the summary related to betrayals. Cheating is one of the most painful types of deception and it can destroy a long-lasting relationship. For example, the story of Tom and Jessica, a young couple from London, illustrates how lies can accumulate and lead to serious consequences.

Tom hid his communication with a colleague, then at first it was just an innocent friendly correspondence. But later his sympathy for this colleague grew, and he began to lie to Jessica more and more to hide his emotional betrayal. When the deception was revealed, Jessica felt deeply hurt, not only that Tom was spending time with another woman, but also that he was not honest with her. The loss was believed to be more devastating than the betrayal itself.

A lie of this level can have serious psychological consequences for both parties. For someone who lies, this often means living in constant stress and fear of being exposed. Such stress can lead to depression, anxiety and even the development of addictions. On the other hand, someone who has become a victim of deception often experiences shock, emotional trauma and loses the ability to trust not only the partner, but also other people in the future.

However, lying in a relationship is not always the result of malicious intent or a desire to harm the other. If she calls because of fear of being vulnerable, because of social pressure or expectations we put on ourselves. For example, John, a successful manager from New York, for a long time did not tell his team that he had problems at work, then he was afraid of losing the image of a "successful man". His lie was not dictated by the desire to deceive his wife, but arose from the fear of disappointing her. He believed that if he told the truth, their relationship might suffer. But, as often happens, you feel the traces of a lie much worse than the truth itself.

The difference between a "white lie" and serious cheating in a relationship can be subtle. What for one person is a small lie, for another - a betrayal of trust. For example, hiding financial problems or downplaying important events in a partner's life can also lead to devastating consequences. Stories like how people lie about their income or expenses to avoid misunderstandings may seem trivial, but it's often these "little lies" that destroy long-lasting relationships.

Long-term education of the truth makes a person vulnerable to further major deceptions and leads to emotional distance between partners.

Psychology professor Deborah Tonkins studied the impact of small deceptions on relationships and concluded that even the smallest forms of lies can accumulate over time and lead to mistrust. Her research shows that when people begin to lie in a relationship, they gradually become distant from each other, which can eventually lead to the breakup of the relationship. People who make small excuses move more easily over time to more serious forms of deception, after each successful deception strengthens the belief that it is safe and will not have consequences.

However, it is important to remember that lying is not only a personal choice, but also a social phenomenon. Modern society, with its demands for success, beauty, and perfection, creates an environment in which people often feel the need to lie in order to meet the expectations of others. Social networks, in particular, play a significant role in shaping such expectations. We see idealized images of other people's lives and begin to feel pressure to live up to those ideals, even if it requires us to hide the truth.

So different types of lies in relationships can be more effective, from small excuses that don't seem to hurt, to betrayal that can destroy a relationship. But in every case, lying has its consequences. Regardless of motive or substance, there is bound to be some loss of trust, and rebuilding that trust can take considerable effort.

Interest in this issue is not only academic. In real life, everyone faces ethical dilemmas when choosing between truth and deception, especially in relationships. Society continues to discuss this topic, and each new one in life demonstrates that honesty in relationships is important – even if it means being vulnerable or facing conflict.

Psychological studies of deception for both parties

Cheating in a relationship is not enough to pass without a trace. Also, if it seems small and insignificant, the psychological research for both parties can be serious and profound. Research shows that lying often causes anxiety, guilt, and ultimately lower self-esteem for the cheater. Those who have been cheated face mistrust, emotional vulnerability and, in some cases, trauma.

Imagine the peace of mind when one partner cheats on the other due to an unknown financial issue. At first glance, it may seem like a small thing: a person does not want to worry his partner, and therefore hides the fact of a loan or debt. But what will happen when the truth comes out? The deceived party not only loses trust in the partner, but also feels betrayed, even if the problem was not really significant. Feelings of emotional stress and mistrust can have a long-term impact on relationships.

One of the important psychological consequences of deception is the formation of an "emotional gap." Lying creates distance between people, even if they continue to communicate. Each new lie undermines the foundation of the relationship, creating an invisible barrier that makes open and honest communication difficult.

This phenomenon can be illustrated by a story from the life of one couple from England. Laura and James had been married for over ten years, but when Laura realized that her husband had been secretly seeing her ex-partner at "friendly" dinners, she felt betrayed, even though James insisted it was just a hookup with no romantic motives . . After this discovery, Laura could not trust James as before. Daily interaction became tense, and Laura doubted his words and actions. The emotional distance between them grew day by day, leading to estrangement and gradual emotional isolation.

From the point of view of psychology, deception often provokes "cognitive dissonance" - an internal conflict between what a person knows is right and what he does. By cheating, a person enters into a struggle with his own conscience, which affects feelings of guilt and emotional stress. Studies show that liars experience a higher level of anxiety, which negatively affects their mental state and physical health.

For example, an experiment by psychologist Robert Feldman, which explored the interaction between lying and well-being, showed that people who lie often have higher levels of stress, which in time can lead to physical problems, from increased blood pressure to weakened immune systems.

However, cheating affects not only the perpetrator, but also the victim. Trust is the foundation of any healthy relationship. When a person sees that they have been deceived, it undermines their ability to believe not only in the person who lied, but also in people in general. After revealing the lie, the victim may become a reason to avoid open communication or even feel afraid of new relationships, which makes further life much more difficult.

Using the example of the famous American psychologist and therapist John Gottman, he describes the story of a couple where the husband brought up problems at work in order not to disturb his wife. She saw this only when the family faced financial difficulties. Although the husband explained his desire to act to protect her from stress, for the wife it was a huge blow to their marriage. She felt excluded from important aspects of their lives, and this undermined her confidence in their future together.

The long-term effects of lying

Constant deception can lead to mental disorders. Victims of lies often experience depression, anxiety, and emotional instability. A person may become less open to new relationships or even lose faith in himself. Psychologists claim that after long-term deception, people develop a sense of ongoing doubt that even in cases of honest relationships, it will be difficult for them to believe in the sincerity of their partner.

In addition, long-term lying can lead to the formation of addictions or compulsive behavior. People who frequently cheat may use it as a defense mechanism or to avoid a problem. This, in turn, can lead to even greater difficulties in the relationship.

Interestingly, Harvard Medical School research shows that people who actively cheat often lose emotional connection with their own behavior. In other words, constant lying dulls moral sense and empathy, which can turn a person into a "cold" manipulator, unable to realize the harm of his actions.

How lying affects physical health

Deception is not limited to emotional or moral impact - it can affect a person's physical health. Studies have shown that constant lying leads to chronic stress, which in its case can cause cardiovascular diseases, high blood pressure and weakened immunity. People who are regularly deceived or lied to are more likely to experience sleep problems, headaches, and other physical symptoms of stress.

Among the interesting studies in this area was the study of psychologist Anna Schneider, which showed that people who avoid lying for a certain time experience an improvement not only in relationships, but also in physical well-being. During the experiment, the participants were asked to avoid any lies for two weeks. As a result, participants noted that their stress levels worsened, they began to sleep better, and they also noticed an improvement in their relationships with others.

Psychological injuries from lying

Psychologists also note that one of the most important forms of trauma associated with deception is the betrayal of a loved one. When we are deceived by people whom we trusted, it creates a big nerve wound that is difficult to heal. Such traumas can accompany a person throughout life, forming behavioral patterns that affect future relationships.

Dr. Linda Freeman, a well-known therapist from California, works with many patients who have survived marital infidelity. She notes that such patients often have problems trusting new partners, even if they demonstrate openness and honesty. Dr. Linda Freeman also notes that the trauma of betrayal can affect not only romantic relationships, but all other human interactions. Those who have survived deception often unconsciously begin to look for subterfuge in any relationship, be it friendship, professional contacts or family relationships. Suspicion and mistrust can become protective mechanisms, but at the same time they prevent people from building healthy and sincere relationships.

One of the most vivid stories about the destructive consequences of lying is the famous case of Enron, an American energy corporation that went bankrupt in 2001 due to a large-scale financial fraud. For years, company leaders hid the real state of affairs from their investors and employees, resorting to lies and manipulation of financial reports. The result: thousands of people lost their jobs, their retirement savings, and their trust in the corporate system in general.

For Enron employees, this crisis was not only a financial blow. Many of them faced a deep sense of betrayal and inner belief in their own competence and significance. Research has shown that after such a crisis, people often lose the ability to build trusting relationships in the workplace and in their personal lives. Many former Enron employees learned that even through the company's bankruptcy, they felt constant anxiety about the financial stability and integrity of their new employers.

How lies change social dynamics

Returning to psychological research, it is worth noting that lying also changes social relations in a larger sense. Not only personal relationships follow from deception, but social institutions also lose trust. As the Enron case shows, a financial crisis caused by high-level lies can lead to distrust of the entire economic system. This supports social stability as people become less trusting of corporations, government agencies, and even justice.

In social psychology, this phenomenon is often called "crisis trust". In today's world, disinformation spreads rapidly through media and social networks, and every big lie resonates far more deeply than ever before. As a result, we face an epidemic of mistrust, where any falsehood—regardless of its scale—maintains a level of faith in people and societal general institutions.

This is supported by another interesting study conducted by psychologist Paul Pife, which found that even small acts of deception, such as lying about minor achievements or increasing personal gains, can eventually lead to a person beginning to perceive lying as socially acceptable behavior. If society tolerates exchange at the level of individual interactions, it will lead to the degradation of social norms.

Lying as an individual and social threat

Cheating can be both a personal matter and a collective problem. At the individual level, it destroys trust, undermines self-esteem, provokes anxiety and depression, and at the social level, it causes a crisis of confidence in entire institutions. A person who has become a victim of lies can lose faith not only in others, but also in his own abilities to build healthy relationships.

A lie changes not only a person's mental state, but also his physical health. It provokes chronic stress, lowers immunity and absorbs general well-being. Long-term studies of deception can manifest in emotional instability, mistrust of other people, and even social isolation.

In addition, in today's world, lies at the corporate and social levels can cause a global crisis of confidence. This further emphasizes that cheating is not only a personal problem, but also a social threat that has long-term consequences for the entire society.

Understanding the psychological and social consequences of deception will help us better understand why honesty and trust are fundamental principles for building healthy relationships and a sustainable society.

How communication can help avoid cheating.

Communication is one of the most powerful tools to avoid cheating in a relationship, whether personal or professional. Open dialogue, honesty and mutual understanding are the foundations on which future trust between people rests. However, many people underestimate the importance of effective communication, which often deteriorates and sometimes leads to deception.

To avoid situations where lying becomes the only way out for one of the parties, it is necessary to learn and use strategies that make communication transparent, honest and constructive.

Why we avoid frank conversations

Often lies are not motivated by the desire to manipulate, but by the fear of being misunderstood or judged. People are afraid that their truth may be perceived painfully, or that it will lead to conflicts. For example, in relationships with friends or partners, people may nurture their true opinions to avoid mistakes or offense. However, instead of promoting peace, such behavior only complicates the damage.

The story of the famous British entrepreneur John is a great example of how failure to communicate honestly can lead to trouble. He was a successful manager of a medium-sized business and had a great relationship with his team. But when the company began to face financial difficulties, John decided to hide it from his employees, hoping that he would be able to quickly solve the problem of the disease. A few months later, it became known that the company was on the verge of bankruptcy, and the employees felt a deep sense of betrayal at not being told the truth.

This situation could have turned out differently if John had explained the real state of affairs to his team in time. Perhaps they found a solution together, and the atmosphere of trust in the team was not affected.

Simple steps to openness

The key to avoiding deception is learning to be honest, even when the truth seems difficult or unpleasant. There are several strategies that can help ensure open and honest communication:

Listen without judging . When a person feels judged, they are more likely to try to hide something or change their illness. Creating a safe environment where everyone can speak up without fear of judgment enhances open conversations.

Express your thoughts and feelings clearly . When a person understands that they are being watched, and that they are, they are less likely to choose lies as a way of avoiding responsibility. For example, in a romantic relationship, a clear discussion of expectations, values, and boundaries will help avoid situations where one party may be tempted to lie.

Explain your intentions . When we explain not only what we think, but also why it is important to us, it reduces the risk that the other person will feel the need to hide the truth.

Regular feedback . Constant conversations about the condition help to avoid the accumulation of misunderstandings. For example, in the work team, regular meetings where successes and difficulties are discussed help to avoid lying for fear of appearing incompetent.

Effective communication strategies

In his book "Why We Lie", the famous psychologist Dan Ariely explains that many people try to lie to avoid conflicts or feelings of guilt. However, as soon as you work on open communication, the motivation to lie decreases.

An important aspect of effective communication is the ability to be vulnerable. People who are ready to talk openly about their fears, failures and weaknesses are less likely to lie. This is confirmed by the psychological research of Professor Brené Brown, which showed that vulnerability is key to building trust.

A great example is the story of a married couple from California who decided to deal with problems in their relationship through a system of open dialogue. They established a rule of "5 minutes of honesty", where everyone had 5 minutes every day to talk openly about their experiences, fears and doubts. This simple ritual helped them avoid lying because of the fear of offending or not being understood.

Why honesty is an investment in a relationship

Honesty is not just a moral obligation, but also an investment in a long-term relationship. When a partner or colleague knows they can expect you to be honest, it builds a solid foundation of trust. When trust is built, any difficulties or conflicts are resolved much easier.

One of the most interesting examples demonstrating this principle is the story of the famous American politician George Washington. According to legend, when he was still a child, he was caught cutting down a cherry tree. When his father asked him about it, George confessed without hesitation, saying, "I can't lie." This simple act of candor later became a symbol of the integrity on which his entire career rested.

CHAPTER 5

How to spot a lie

Strategies for recognizing lies (speech signals, non-verbal signs).

Communication built on openness and honesty can be a reliable strategy for avoiding lies. Therefore, it is important to remember that for many, even when the truth seems painful or unwanted, it is always better than a lie, after which it strengthens trust and builds deeper relationships.

When it comes to lie detection, there are many tools and techniques that help detect deception. The most obvious signs are the verbal and non-verbal cues that people may give when they are lying. However, detecting lies is a complex process that requires attention to detail, observation and intuition.

Speech signals

Language is the first thing we pay attention to when trying to understand whether a person is telling the truth. Often, even if we have good control over your non-verbal responses, our words can convey more than we intend.

One of the first signals is strong detail or, on the contrary, too general answers. A liar may add too many details to make his illness more convincing. For example, if someone asks where you were last night and you say something like, "I was at the coffee shop on the corner, I ordered a late soy milk because they ran out of regular milk, and then I had to wait ten minutes ". ", this may be a sign that you are trying to convince the interlocutor of the truth of your words.

Another extended speech signal is avoidance of a direct response. Liars often remember evasive phrases like "If I remember correctly" or "Maybe it was like that." Such phrases not only create a feeling of insecurity, but also give the liar room to maneuver in case of exposure.

Non-verbal signs

Nonverbal communication is another important indicator of authenticity. It often gives away our emotions faster than we realize it. One of the classic examples of nonverbal signs of lying is microexpressions. These are fleeting emotions that appear on a person's face literally for a fraction of a second and may indicate that he is experiencing a certain stress or internal contradiction.

Professor Paul Ekman, an expert on emotions and micro viruses, will eventually help develop a lie detection system based on micro viruses. He claims that even the most skilled liars cannot fully control these small facial features. For example, a person can smile, but the micro-viscera that appears on the face before or after the smile can show his true state - fear, anger or despair.

Another interesting non-verbal signal is the incompatibility of words and gestures. For example, if a person says "Yes, I agree" but at the same time nods his head in the direction of "no", this may be a sign that he is lying. It is also worth paying attention to small movements, such as picking the nose, looking away or covering the mouth with a hand during a conversation - all these can indicate discomfort and possible lying.

Pause strategy

Another accidental signal of a lie is the use of pauses while speaking. People who lie often pause before answering a question to make up a plausible illness. Lying researcher Dr. David Christle found that liars typically have longer pauses between questions and answers, especially if the question is unexpected. At the same time, answering too quickly without a pause can also indicate the preparation of lies in advance.

An interesting real-life example can be taken from the story of Richard Nixon and his famous press conference during the Watergate scandal. When reporters asked Nixon about his possible involvement in the conspiracy, he didn't pause before saying, "I'm not a crook." His too-quick response, in which he unhesitatingly defended his reputation, became critical for many experts who study lies. And as time has shown, in this situation Nixon was indeed not telling the truth.

Emotions and uniqueness

Lying is often accompanied by incompleteness in emotional reactions. This can be determined in the way a person expresses his emotions about the situations he is talking about. For example, if a person talks about a tragic event, but at the same time looks too calm or even smiles, it can be said that he does not feel the emotions that he is trying to convey.

A good example of this can be seen in the famous case of Amanda Knox. When she was questioned about the murder of her roommate in Italy, investigators noticed that her emotional reactions seemed 'out of place.' In the video, she often smiled and showed no signs of remorse or shock, which appeared unusual. This attracted the attention of the press and raised suspicions about her involvement. Although she was eventually acquitted, her behavior during interrogations has long remained a topic of debate.

Strategic use of questions

One of the most effective lie detection techniques is the use of well-asked questions. It is important to ask unexpected questions that are not related to the main topic of the conversation to see the person's reaction. For example, during criminal investigations, investigators often use the tactic of "indirect questions." If a person is lying, it will be difficult for them to respond quickly to these questions, because they are busy maintaining their main false story.

How to train the ability to recognize lies

If you want to better understand when they are trying to deceive you, you should pay attention not only to words, but also to non-verbal signals, emotions and pauses in conversations. Try to start with small experiments. During daily conversations, train observation, analyze how interlocutors answer questions, whether their emotions correspond to the topic of conversation.

One of the interesting experiments conducted by scientists in Oxford showed that people who trained their ability to notice microexpressions and analyze non-verbal signals were 30% more likely to recognize lies than those who did not have such training.

Of course, not everyone can become a professional lie detector, but these basic strategies allow you to better understand people's behavior and minimize the risk of being deceived.

With the development of technology, new possibilities for detecting lies are opening up. Voice analysis technologies, originally used for military purposes, are gaining popularity in business and law enforcement. Voice analysis software can detect the slightest changes in tone, speed, and volume of speech that can indicate emotional stress or insincerity. One of the included studies found that voice algorithms could determine the level of stress associated with cheating with an accuracy of up to 70%. For example, a company uses such a program during a telephone interview to check whether a candidate is answering truthfully.

In addition, artificial intelligence allows you to analyze video recordings of conversations, knowing microexpressions that are difficult to notice with the human eye. Microexpressions are momentary facial muscle contractions that can reveal true emotions even when a person is trying to hide them. Such technologies are already used in airports to analyze the behavior of passengers during inspection or questioning.

Another important aspect of lie detection is cultural differences. Behavior that may indicate insincerity in one culture may be a simple gesture of courtesy in another. For example, in some Asian countries, making eye contact during a conversation is considered rude and can show respect, while in Western cultures avoiding eye contact is often seen as a sign of deception. This highlights the importance of considering the cultural context when trying to detect lies.

An interesting psychological phenomenon is the so-called cognitive load, which accompanies lies. When a person lies, he is forced to remember two parallel versions of events: real and fictional. This creates additional burdens on her mind, due to the fact that liars often make unique confirmations or easily get confused in their own words. For example, lawyers often use this tactic in trials, asking a lot of probing questions to see if the defendant can follow your side of the story.

A classic example from the English-speaking world is the case of Lance Armstrong, a famous cyclist who was accused of doping. for years he successfully lied to deny all the allegations, but in various interviews his non-verbal cues began to show preference. Subsequently, during one of the interviews, he made a number of linguistic inconsistencies and avoided direct answers, which gave rise to a deeper investigation. Armstrong often paused before answering, avoided clear eye contact, and tried to shift responsibility to others, raising doubts about his sincerity. As a result, he was exposed and banned from all his titles.

It is impossible to ignore ethical aspect in the process of recognizing lies. There is a fine line between the desire to find the truth and moral responsibility for the methods used. For example, the use of the polygraph, although it has proven to be an effective tool, can put a person under a lot of sensitive pressure, even if they are telling the truth. Such methods also often leave personal privacy in doubt and can be misused.

Finally, it is worth remembering practical tips for spotting lies in everyday life. Pay attention to body language: unnatural hand positions, partial face touching, avoiding eye contact, or even strong eye contact can all be signs of stress. At the same time, it is important to understand that such a sign is not direct evidence of a lie, but only indicators that require further analysis.

For example, in family life, a partner who answers a question insincerely may avoid elaborate answers or try to change the subject. However, this does not always mean deception, but can indicate fatigue, stress or even a loss of interest in a certain topic. Therefore, it is important in such cases not to rush to conclusions, but to calmly and openly discuss your beliefs.

Thus, lie detection strategies are a complex combination of technology, psychological techniques, and ethical approaches. The ability to correctly interpret non-verbal signals, understand the cognitive load on a person, as well as get cultural differences can significantly help in the process of exposing deception.

Tests and techniques that verify the veracity of information.

Verification of the truth of information is an important tool for modern society, especially in a world where we are constantly faced with a large flow of information from various sources. There are many techniques and tests that help verify the validity of data to avoid manipulation and misinformation.

One of the most common methods is fact checking, or fact-checking. This approach has become popular in political debates, the media, and even social media, where misinformation spreads at breakneck speed. Fact-checking consists of analyzing statements, checking them with reliable sources, and drawing conclusions about whether they are true. For example, during election campaigns, journalists and independent organizations conduct fact-checking of candidates' statements, comparing them with official statistical data and previous performances.

An interesting story about this happened in the USA in 2016, when during a debate of one of the candidates, his statements about the economic indicators of the country were refuted less than an hour after the speech. Fact-checking teams used online data to quickly verify his words, and the media quickly reported the discrepancy.

Reverse image search is another simple but powerful tool for verifying the veracity of information. It allows you to detect whether an image distributed on the Internet is original or used out of context, manipulated or falsified. Image manipulation is often used to create fake news that preys on people's emotions. You can use tools like Google Reverse Image Search or TinEye to do this.

One of the more advanced techniques is content analysis, which involves examining the text or message for certain patterns or indicators of false information. This may include analyzing stylistic features, the frequency of using emotionally charged words, or the use of uncertain sources. It is known that manipulators often use vague formulations such as "experts say", "sources confirm" without specific references to sources. Artificial intelligence technologies are already able to analyze large volumes of text and automatically highlight those messages that have a higher probability of being false.

One such example was in a media campaign exposing fake news about Brexit in the UK. Algorithms were able to analyze hundreds of thousands of messages on social networks to identify patterns typical of disinformation campaigns. This enabled the government to react in time and warn citizens about the risk of spreading false data.

Polygraph, or "lie detector", is perhaps the most famous technique for checking truthfulness, although not the most reliable. It is based on measuring physiological responses, such as changes in heart rate, breathing and electrical skin resistance, when a person is asked about certain facts. The basic idea is that when a person lies, their body reacts to it with stress. However, polygraphs have their limitations. Emotionally stable people or trained liars can learn to control their reactions and thus cheat the polygraph. Therefore, the results of such tests are not always accepted in court as irrefutable evidence.

Socratic method, which comes from the philosopher Socrates, is another effective way to detect falsehood. It consists in asking a series of logical questions in order to identify contradictions in a person's statements. This method is often used by lawyers during cross-examination, when they are trying to get the accused to come clean. Repeated questioning forces a person to think about their answers, and if they lie, it often leads to mistakes or inconsistencies.

In one case in England, a well-known lawyer used this method during a fraud trial. He carefully examined the testimony of the witness, asking questions about trifles. At first the witness seemed confident, but with each new question his answers became more contradictory, which led to the fact that his lies were exposed in court.

It is no less interesting **metadata analysis**, which is especially useful in the age of digital technologies. Metadata is information contained "behind the scenes" of files and messages, such as creation date, authorship, geographic location, and even modification history. For example, in investigative journalism cases, it is often useful to analyze the metadata of photos and videos to verify when and where they were taken. In 2017, journalists from a British newspaper exposed the false statements of one political figure by analyzing the metadata of his photos. It turned out that the image, which was supposed to confirm his presence at an important meeting, was taken in a completely different place and time.

Also worth mentioning **cognitive tests**, which are used to detect discrepancies in human memory. These tests are based on the fact that truthful information is usually better remembered, while lies may seem less detailed or change over time. One such test is to ask a person to re-describe the same event some time later and compare the responses for changes or inconsistencies.

Thus, in today's world there are many tests and techniques that allow you to check the veracity of information. The use of modern technologies, psychological methods and traditional approaches, such as the Socratic method, makes it possible to more effectively separate truth from lies.

Recommendations for the analysis of information sources.

Analysis of information sources has become a place in today's world, where the volume of available data is constantly growing. We receive information every day from numerous sources: news sites, social networks, blogs and other online platforms. However, no skin source is reliable, and the ability to distinguish true information from manipulation can protect us from misinformation and false beliefs.

One of the key principles in source analysis is critical thinking . This means that you should not accept information as truth just because it sounds good or comes from a reputable source. Also important media can make mistakes or distort facts in pursuit of sensationalism. For example, in the 1990s, a newspaper *The New*

York Times published a series of articles about a man they called a "working-class hero." But after a few years, it turned out that most of these stories were made up. The newspaper later published a rebuttal, but the damage from the misinformation had already been done.

There are some practical tips for checking sources. First of all, pay attention to the authority of the source . Is the author of the article an expert in your field? What is the reputation of the source? For example, scientific journals are reviewed by other experts, so their materials often have a higher level of credibility. On the other hand, private blogs can express subjective opinions without proper fact-checking.

independence of authority, it is also important to take into account accuracy and relevance of the source . Does the provided information agree with other known facts? Imagine that you are reading news about medical research. Check multiple sources and see if they cite original scientific works. One of the most prominent examples of successful use of this approach occurred in the UK, when a research team used data from multiple independent sources to debunk fake news about a scientific breakthrough. This became the post office for new standards of verification of scientific data in the media.

Publication time also matters. Information may become outdated or lose its relevance. So before you trust a source, make sure it's up to date. Old studies may not yield new scientific discoveries, and new reports sometimes change as new facts emerge.

Objectivity of the source — another important aspect. Ask yourself: Could the author have a vested interest or bias? It is not necessarily known about lies, but you should be careful with information that appears too one-sided. For example, during political problems, the media may favor one party, distorting the facts in favor of its success.

exclusively the above criteria, it is important to understand that fact checking can not always be again. Sometimes, in order to verify the veracity of certain information, it is necessary to refer to several different sources, analyze them, compare them, and conduct additional research.

A real story from the world of British media may illustrate this point. In one of the investigations, which appeared on the BBC in 2010, journalists tried to expose corruption in the state structure. They received an anonymous source who provided documents that confirmed widespread abuse. Protest, before publishing the material, journalists check these data through independent verified sources. Apparently, the documents were a forgery created by competitors in order to discredit a government official. Such careful analysis avoids the publication of false information that could harm innocent people.

Technologies also play an important role in the source verification process. Nowadays, artificial intelligence and algorithms can quickly analyze large volumes of data, locate inconsistencies and detect false information. Fact-checking programs have already become part of the toolkit of many journalists. However, it should be noted that technology is not perfect, and the human factor remains decisive.

A true story from the English world can also help to better understand, it is important to be critical of the sources. In 2003, a British newspaper *The Guardian* published an investigation that later became known as the "Spy Letters Affair". It was about allegedly genuine documents that confirmed Great Britain's espionage against one of its allies. The newspaper, referring to these letters, wrote a series of articles that caused an international scandal. However, after some time it turned out that the documents were forged, and their source used these data for manipulation. Later *The Guardian* apologized for the publication, admitting errors in its source verification. This situation is a stark example of how even the most respected media outlets can be vulnerable to misinformation if they don't do enough vetting of sources.

Etika follows an important role in the process of analyzing information sources. This especially applies to journalists, scientists and other professionals whose activities are related to the transmission of information to a wide audience. Spreading false or unverified information can lead to serious consequences. For example, journalists are required to adhere to ethical standards, not only with facts, but also by protecting their sources and not violating other people's rights.

Thus, the analysis of information sources is a critical dominance that allows us to make informed decisions and protect against manipulation. Critical thinking, fact-checking, analyzing the objectivity and credibility of sources, and the use of technology are just some of the key tools that help us distinguish between truth and lies. Real-life stories, as coincidental with British media, highlight the importance of these skills in today's world, where information is crucial to shaping our reality.

Analysis of information sources is a tool in the fight against disinformation. In this day and age, when information is available in seconds, critical thinking and media literacy remain integral parts of our ubiquitous lives. As we have already discussed, proper analysis can prevent the influence of false information, but it is also important to pay attention to the new challenges we face.

The influence of the social network on the information landscape

Social networks such as Facebook, Twitter and Instagram have changed the way we receive and store information. Now practically everyone has the opportunity to become a source of news, which, on the one hand, expands opportunities, and on the other hand, significantly complicates the process of fact-checking. One of the most high-profile examples is the disinformation campaign during the 2016 US election. Then, fake news spread through social networks, influencing the minds of voters.

Such situations indicate the need for a critical approach to information consumption. Social networks not only shape our information space, but also often lead to the emergence of "information bubbles" in which users only receive information that confirms their views. This limits their perception of diversity of opinion and creates a warning that may in time negatively affect public discourse.

Examples of fact-checking

Fortunately, in response to the spread of misinformation, there is a fact-checking initiative. Organizations such as Snopes and FactCheck.org do important work verifying the veracity of information shared on the Internet. such resources have become one of the reference points for those who want to distinguish truth from falsehood.

One example of a successful campaign is a program implemented in schools. Students are taught to critically evaluate information, they are taught to look for facts and draw conclusions based on evidence. The methods involved include group discussions, analysis of various sources of information, and practical exercises to detect fake news.

The role of media literacy

Media literacy is another important aspect to focus on. In countries such as Sweden, media literacy has become an integral part of the curriculum, where students learn to analyze and evaluate sources of information. Thus, the Swedish model provides interactive concepts that stimulate students to actively discuss the topic of disinformation, contributing to the formation of citizens' consciousness.

Psychological aspects

There are no less psychological aspects of information perception. People often believe what supports their personality beliefs—a phenomenon known as confirmation bias. When information appears on social networks that supports certain political or social views, users become more popular as it is recognized as true. This can lead to further polarization of society as different groups begin to live in their own "information worlds".

INit is important to emphasize that analyzing information sources is a necessary skill in today's world. Increasing media literacy, critical thinking and the use of technologies to check facts become a guarantee of objectivity in the information space. Readers should remember that real knowledge is not only information, but also the ability to analyze and evaluate it. Only in this way can we be sure of the truthfulness of what surrounds us and contribute to the formation of a healthy information environment.

These reflections and actions can help each of us become a more conscious consumer of information, which is at home in the fight against misinformation in our lives.

CHAPTER 6

Ethics and the Future

Can some forms of lying be justified?

When it comes to lying, the question arises whether some forms of untruth can be justified. In our world, where moral and ethical norms often collide with practical realities, understanding this issue becomes especially important. Sometimes circumstances can seem so critical that people feel the need to resort to lying to achieve certain goals. Let's consider in what situations it can be justified, and what psychological and social mechanisms can influence such decisions.

One of the most discussed forms of justifying lies is the "noble lie." This term describes situations where lying is done to protect or help others. An example of such a situation can be the case of the outstanding English doctor Frederick Trent, who worked in a hospital in the 1970s. He often encountered patients who were diagnosed with incurable diseases. Realizing that his patients were losing hope because of the harsh truth, he began to use careful wording and gentle words that helped patients cope with their fears. Trent believed that by teaching patients to live in the moment and hope for the best, he could give them some joy in their final days.

It's important to note that while noble lies may be well-intentioned, they can also lead to complications. In situations like Trent's, patients can feel cheated if they learn the truth later. This begs the question: is it worth resorting to lying, even if the intentions are good? The answer to this question is not clear. Each case requires an individual analysis, and here it is important to pay attention to the ethical framework.

The next example that illustrates this point is a security situation. In 2001, during terrorist attacks in the USA, British security services received information about possible threats. In order to avoid panic among the population, the authorities decided to hide some of the information that could cause fear and uncertainty. This caused heated discussions about the justification of such a step. On the one hand, preventing mass panic seemed logical, but on the other hand, citizens have the right to know the truth about their safety.

This conflict between security and the right to information illustrates a broader social phenomenon. Sociological research suggests that people are willing to accept some forms of lying if they believe it leads to well-being or security. However, there is always the risk that such lies may have unforeseeable consequences that may threaten the trust between citizens and the authorities.

Technology also plays an important role in this debate. In today's world of instant information, decisions about what to say and when to say it can have significant consequences. For example, if a government chooses to withhold information about cyber threats to avoid panic, it may face criticism for a lack of transparency. On the other hand, the lack of information can lead to mass fear if the problem becomes known through other channels.

Psychological aspects should not be ignored either. People often believe what they want to believe. This is supported by the concept of "confirmation bias," which suggests that people tend to seek out and interpret information that confirms their preexisting beliefs. In such a context, some may believe that lying is not only a means of protection, but also a way of avoiding discomfort.

Technologies in this case can both support and deny this illusion. Social media algorithms that personalize content for each user can create information bubbles where people only receive information that is relevant to their views. This makes it more likely that users will accept a lie as truth if it is consistent with their beliefs.

In addition, the ethical issues surrounding lying also require attention. For example, journalists are always faced with a dilemma:

should they disclose certain information if it could harm a person or group of people? This issue can become especially relevant in cases where the confidentiality of information sources is discussed. Journalists' codes of ethics are often tested when it comes to deciding whether concealing certain facts is a form of exculpation or irresponsibility.

In conclusion, the question of the justification of lies is complex and multifaceted. Each case requires an individual approach, taking into account the circumstances, intentions, consequences and ethical standards. Can some forms of lying be justified? This question remains open. It is important to consider all these factors when analyzing the situation, and also to understand that our actions can always have both positive and negative consequences. The true ability to discern when and how to lie depends on our values, beliefs, and willingness to take responsibility for our actions.

Lies can take many forms, and our task is to understand how they affect us and our society, and how we can learn to distinguish truth from falsehood in the complex maze of modern life.

How can technology change our understanding of truth in the future?

Technology is rapidly changing our lives, and with it comes a new challenge to our understanding of truth. The question of how these technologies can affect our perception of truth in the future is becoming more and more relevant. From social media to artificial intelligence, new tools are shaping our thoughts, influencing our decisions, and may even cause significant social disruption. Let's look at how technology can change our understanding of truth.

One of the main factors to consider is information dissemination. In today's world, anyone can become a source of news thanks to social networks. This availability of information opens new horizons, but also creates a threat. For example, in 2016, during the US presidential election, fake news was actively spread through Facebook and Twitter. Many people believed what they read without checking the facts, which led to the spread of misinformation. In the future, with the development of technology, new methods of detecting false information may appear, but the volume of manipulation may also increase.

Artificial intelligence (AI) is another powerful tool that will affect our perception of truth. Thanks to learning algorithms, AI can analyze a large amount of data and determine parental behavior for human purposes. For example, companies that use AI to personalize ads can analyze your preferences to create ads that are best suited to you. However, this can lead to the creation of "information bubbles" in which users will only leave information that confirms their pre-existing belief. It can limit our horizons and make us believe that certain views are the only correct ones, even when they are not.

It is also worth thinking about technologies related to virtual and augmented reality. In the future, these technologies can become powerful through manipulation. Imagine that instead of watching the usual news, you could be in the center of events, immersed in virtual reality. While this can improve our understanding of events, it can also create opportunities for misinformation. For example, virtual images or scenarios can be manipulated to show certain emotions and, as a result, make people believe something that is far from reality.

The psychological aspect is also important in this context. Modern technologies can use manipulation methods based on psychology. For example, social media can create an environment that encourages people to share certain views or news, while others, less popular, may go unnoticed. It is a risk that the perception of truth becomes unique for each individual, depending on his personal preferences and information sources.

In addition, ethical issues related to technology will play a key role in our understanding of truth. What ethical standards should govern the use of technologies for data collection and analysis? How can people be protected from manipulation? For example, with the development of biometric technologies that can detect emotions, the question arises: should companies be allowed to use such data for entire advertising or political empowerment?

This all brings us to thinking about how we can prepare for these changes in the future. One of the possible solutions can be education. Citizens must be educated on how to critically evaluate information, recognize manipulation, and understand how technology can affect their perception of the truth. Media education programs can be a step in ensuring information literacy.

In addition, the development of technologies for fact-checking and combating disinformation will be critical. There are already projects that use artificial intelligence to verify information in real time. For example, some platforms apply new algorithms to determine whether the news is true or fake. However, it is important to remember that no technology is perfect, so you should always remain critical.

We must not forget about the role of governments and regulators. Legislative initiatives can help manage the spread of misinformation and protect consumer rights. For example, the European Union has already introduced laws that oblige social networks to verify the information published on their platforms.

So, as technology advances, our understanding of truth may change, but it depends on how we use it. Will we be open to new knowledge, or will we allow technology to shape our perception of reality? Society must find a balance between technological advances and critical thinking to maintain a true understanding of truth in an ever-changing world.

Ultimately, while technology can change our understanding of truth, the key is how we relate to it. Can we adapt to these changes while remaining critical and conscious? This is the question we face in the near future. And the answer to it can shape how we perceive the truth in a world filled with dangers.

Potential scenarios of the development of the situation with lies in society.

Potential scenarios of the development of the situation with lies in society have become especially relevant in the conditions of rapid development of technologies and growth of information flow. Modern society faces low-level challenges related to truth and misinformation. But is it possible to create a more truthful society? To answer this question, let's consider several scenarios.

The first scenario involves the active involvement of citizens in the process of forming public opinion. In conditions where information is constantly circulating in the online space, it is important that people learn to critically evaluate what they read. An example of this is the campaign against fake news, which gained popularity in Great Britain. In 2017, in response to the spread of misinformation during the country's elections, initiatives were introduced to encourage people to check facts before sharing news on social media. Civil society organizations have developed tools to verify information, which has helped to significantly reduce the spread of false information.

The second scenario changes at the level of technology. Modern artificial intelligence algorithms are increasingly being used to check facts. For example, platforms that provide news can automatically analyze posts for fake information, offering users truthful alternatives. This, of course, does not eliminate the problem of disinformation, but it can significantly reduce its impact on society.

However, technology can be a double-edged sword. Modern tools allow not only to detect disinformation, but also to create it. For example, generative neural networks can be used to create fake videos that look completely realistic. The situation can become complicated if such technology falls into the hands of people with bad intentions. In this context, it is important to understand that technology itself is not good or bad; their use by ethical norms of society.

The third scenario occurs in the ethical changes in the media industry. Journalists can become active defenders of the truth by promoting ethical standards that require them to verify information and use its context. Increasing news quality standards can reduce the level of misinformation. A clear example of this is the changes that occurred after the Cambridge Analytica scandal, when it was revealed that the data of millions of Facebook users was used to manipulate electoral processes. Since then, many media outlets have begun to question how information can be used and how they should be held accountable for news accuracy.

The fourth scenario may be related to changes in the educational system. In society, disinformation is becoming more and more accessible, critical thinking and media education should become an integral part of the curriculum. An example is the media education program introduced in some British schools, which teaches students how to recognize misinformation and be critical of information sources. This could be another step in creating a more informed society capable of distinguishing truth from falsehood.

However, despite positive changes, society will always face challenges. People may have other motives for receiving information. For example, a psychological phenomenon known as cognitive bias can lead people to ignore facts that are consistent with their beliefs. such prejudice can become an obstacle on the way to a more truthful society. This means that even with the presence of technology and educational initiatives, society cannot completely get rid of misinformation.

An important point in this process is increasing social responsibility. Citizens should be aware that their actions may affect the dissemination of information. For example, simply following through on a promise to verify information before sharing it on social media can significantly reduce misinformation.

In addition, it is necessary to develop communities that encourage the discussion of ideas and views. Participating in such discussions can help people understand different points of view, as well as foster healthy critical thinking. This can include both local meetings and online platforms where people can share their thoughts and verify information.

After all, is it possible to create a more truthful society? The answer to this question is complicated. There is definitely room for improvement, but it will require effort from all of us. Education, ethics, technology, and the consciousness of society — all these factors develop an important role in shaping a more truthful world.

Thus, the key point is to encourage critical thinking. Readers need to learn not only to learn information, but also to analyze it, ask questions and understand why certain information is presented in this way. This can be the first step on the way to a more informed society that is able to resist manipulation and lies. In our agency-saturated world, it's important to remain active news consumers who can discern not only the truth, but also the motives of those providing it. It's time for all of us to learn to be critical of the information we consume and to be responsible for our place in society.

Success stories

In today's world of general misinformation, it is important to understand how some people and the needs of organizations overcome lies and distortions of facts. This success story serves as a vivid example of how the search for truth and transparency can change society for the better. By studying this history, we not only learn from the mistakes of the past, but can also draw inspiration for building a more truthful society in the future.

One such story is the case of British journalist Cameron Pearce, who in 2017 started countering disinformation on social networks. Pearce witnessed how false information about migrants is spread on the Internet, creating a negative attitude towards them. By spotting misinformation, he created a platform that allowed users to fact-check and provide credible sources of information.

Thanks to him, Cameron Pierce was able not only to stop the spread of misinformation but also to help people develop critical thinking. He taught people not only to take information on faith but also to check facts before accepting them as true. His campaign was successful because many people began to consciously approach the choice of information sources, and as a result, negative stereotypes about migrants began to disappear.

Another striking story is the "good news" initiative, which was started by a group of journalists in Great Britain. During one of the biggest crises in the media industry, when misinformation reached incredible proportions, this group decided to create a platform focused on positive news. They understand that the constant flow of negative information only fuels fear and misunderstanding among people. Dubbed the Good News Network, this platform began actively spreading positive stories that inspired people and gave them hope.

Individual journals of this initiative that positive news help to form a more optimistic view of the world and reduce the impact of misinformation. Readers became open to new ideas and possibilities, which, in due time, contributed to the development of a healthy society where everyone was ready to support each other.

However, the success story is not always related only to the media or journalism. In a London school, history teacher Mary Evans noticed that many of her students were unable to critically evaluate information. She decided to change the approach to education, including in the lessons a discussion of disinformation and ways to detect it.

She started a project in which students had to find random misinformation in the news and prepare their own presentations about how and why those facts might be distorted. The project not only increased this student's level of critical thinking, but also helped them to see the importance of choosing reliable sources of information. With this approach, many students have become more critical of the information they consume and have even started discussing it at home with their parents.

Another example is the history of the "Full Fact" organization, which works in Great Britain and specializes in fact-checking. This independent organization was created to help ensure the accuracy of information in society. With dedicated tools and resources, Full Fact works to identify misinformation and provide objective facts.

The organization once collected a huge database that helped not only journalists, but also ordinary citizens to check facts in real time. It has become one of the resources that allows people to detect misinformation in the news, which, in turn, ensures the general level of information of the population.

These success stories show that the fight against misinformation and lies is possible and done. Each of the examples mentioned illustrates how individual efforts can lead to change at a larger level. When people take responsibility for the information they consume and share, they make a significant contribution to creating a more truthful society.

Understanding that truth is not always absolute, but depends on context and the source of information, can help us become more self-aware. By including examples of successful fights against disinformation, we can encourage readers to think critically and independently analyze information. Such thinking becomes a tool in a world where truth is often subject to manipulation.

Countering misinformation requires efforts not only from journalists or organizations, but also from each of us. We can all be a part of this important cause by developing the ability to think critically and check the hidden facts. Thus, by joining our efforts, we can move towards a society based on truth and transparency.

Literary analysis: Truth, Deception, and the Ethical Horizon

Literature has long served as one of humanity's most precise instruments for examining truth and deception. Through narrative, metaphor, and character, writers expose not only *what* people believe, but *why* they choose to believe it—and what happens when truth is bent, rewritten, or erased. In the context of modern society, literary works remain uniquely relevant, offering ethical insight into mechanisms of manipulation that now operate on a technological scale.

George Orwell's *1984* remains one of the most powerful explorations of truth under systemic control. Orwell does not merely depict a society where lies exist; he constructs a world in which truth itself is no longer stable. Through the concept of *doublethink*, individuals are trained to accept contradictions as reality—to believe and disbelieve the same statement simultaneously. This is not simply political propaganda; it is psychological conditioning. Orwell demonstrates how power over language becomes power over thought, and how ethical collapse begins not with violence, but with the quiet erosion of shared reality.

Equally compelling, though less overtly dystopian, are modern literary examinations of subjective truth. In *The Sense of an Ending*, Julian Barnes explores how memory reshapes reality. The novel reveals that deception does not always require malice; often, it emerges from self-protection. Characters rewrite their own past not to manipulate others, but to preserve a coherent identity. Barnes reminds us that truth can fracture internally long before it is distorted externally—a theme profoundly relevant in an age where personal narratives are constantly curated and broadcast.

Contemporary literature repeatedly returns to this tension: truth as an ethical obligation versus truth as a psychological burden. Family dramas, political novels, and social satires illustrate how small distortions—omissions, softened narratives, selective memories—can gradually corrode trust. These stories make visible what statistics and headlines cannot: the emotional cost of living within constructed realities.

In the digital era, these literary insights acquire renewed urgency. Social networks and algorithm-driven platforms now perform functions once reserved for storytellers and editors. They shape narratives, prioritize certain voices, and obscure others. Unlike literature, however, these systems are optimized not for ethical reflection, but for engagement. The result is an environment where emotionally charged misinformation spreads more efficiently than verified truth.

Real-world examples underscore this danger. During recent election cycles in the United Kingdom and elsewhere, false narratives circulated widely before being challenged by independent journalists and fact-checking organizations. These cases reveal both the vulnerability of public discourse and its resilience. While manipulation spreads rapidly, collective ethical response—when supported by critical literacy—can still restore balance.

Algorithms, however, complicate this struggle. By reinforcing existing beliefs and filtering out dissenting information, they create informational echo chambers that mirror Orwellian control without centralized authority. Truth is no longer suppressed by force; it is quietly outcompeted. Ethical responsibility therefore extends beyond individual honesty to structural awareness. Understanding how information is curated becomes as important as evaluating the information itself.

Literature offers an antidote to this passive consumption. Thoughtful reading trains the mind to tolerate ambiguity, recognize bias, and question narrative authority. It encourages readers not merely to absorb meaning, but to interrogate it. In this sense, literature is not an escape from reality, but preparation for it.

The ethical future of truth depends on this capacity for reflection. A society capable of critical reading—of texts, media, and technologies—is better equipped to resist manipulation. Ethical communication requires more than factual accuracy; it demands transparency of intent, accountability of systems, and humility in interpretation.

Truth, ultimately, is not a static possession but an ongoing practice. It requires vigilance, empathy, and the willingness to revise one's understanding in light of new evidence. Literature, psychology, and technology are not opposing forces in this endeavor; when approached responsibly, they become complementary tools.

To move beyond the labyrinth of lies, society must cultivate both intellectual rigor and moral courage. This means questioning comforting narratives, examining the systems that shape perception, and accepting that honesty is often more demanding than deception. The path forward is neither simple nor absolute—but it remains navigable for those willing to think critically, read deeply, and act ethically.

CONCLUSION

Is society possible without lies?

Throughout this book, we have walked through the winding corridors of human deception — from harmless white lies to the calculated manipulations that influence governments, markets, and entire cultures. The question guiding this journey has remained simple yet profound: *Is a society without lies truly possible?*

The honest answer is both uncomfortable and liberating. A world entirely free of lies is unlikely. Deception is deeply embedded in human psychology. It emerges from fear, self-preservation, the desire for acceptance, and sometimes from genuine attempts to protect others from harm. From childhood, people learn to adjust reality to navigate social expectations and emotional complexities. In this sense, lies are not merely moral failures; they are also survival strategies shaped by evolution and social development.

However, while lies may be inevitable, a society dominated by deception is not. The real danger does not lie in the existence of lies, but in the normalization of manipulation and the passive acceptance of distorted truth.

During our exploration, we have seen how deception operates on multiple levels. On a personal scale, dishonesty weakens trust — the fragile yet essential bond that holds relationships together. In professional environments, manipulation can distort decision-making and undermine institutional credibility. On a societal level, misinformation can fracture communities, intensify polarization, and weaken democratic systems that depend on informed and rational public discourse.

The digital age has amplified these challenges. Information now travels faster than reflection. Algorithms shape perception by feeding individuals content that confirms their beliefs, often isolating them inside invisible informational walls. In such environments, truth becomes fragmented, and emotional resonance often outweighs factual accuracy. The result is not only confusion, but also a growing vulnerability to strategic manipulation by those who understand how to exploit attention, fear, and outrage.

Yet this landscape does not condemn society to permanent deception. It reveals a responsibility — one that extends beyond governments, media institutions, or technology companies. The preservation of truth increasingly depends on individuals who are willing to engage actively with information rather than consume it passively.

Critical thinking becomes more than an intellectual exercise; it becomes a form of civic responsibility. To question sources, to analyze motives, and to seek multiple perspectives are not acts of skepticism alone — they are acts of protection. They protect personal autonomy, social stability, and the integrity of public dialogue.

At the same time, critical thinking must be balanced with trust. A society built entirely on suspicion cannot function either. The challenge is not to reject trust, but to develop informed trust — trust supported by transparency, accountability, and evidence. This balance allows individuals to cooperate, build institutions, and maintain social cohesion while remaining resistant to manipulation.

Ethics also play a decisive role in shaping the future of truth. Communication — whether personal, journalistic, or political — forms the moral infrastructure of society. When honesty becomes secondary to profit, power, or influence, public confidence deteriorates. Restoring this confidence requires cultural change. Honesty must be valued not only as a moral ideal but as a practical necessity for sustainable cooperation and progress.

Education represents one of the most powerful tools in this transformation. Teaching people how to evaluate information, recognize persuasive tactics, and understand cognitive biases equips them with intellectual resilience. Media literacy and emotional awareness allow individuals to navigate complex informational environments without becoming overwhelmed or manipulated. Societies that invest in these skills create citizens who are not only informed but also empowered.

Technology, often seen as a source of misinformation, can also become part of the solution. Transparent algorithms, responsible content moderation, and advanced fact-checking systems can reduce the spread of deception. Yet technological safeguards alone are insufficient. Without ethical responsibility and critical awareness among users, even the most advanced systems remain vulnerable to exploitation.

Ultimately, the future of truth depends on a collective choice. Every individual participates in the information ecosystem — as a reader, listener, speaker, and sharer of ideas. Each decision to verify information before sharing it, each willingness to reconsider personal biases, and each effort to communicate honestly contributes to strengthening the social fabric.

The labyrinth of truth is not a place we escape once and for all. It is a landscape we navigate throughout our lives. At times, its corridors are illuminated by clarity and understanding. At other moments, they are clouded by uncertainty and illusion. The goal is not to eliminate every falsehood, but to develop the wisdom and awareness necessary to recognize when we are losing our way.

Truth is rarely simple. It is shaped by context, perspective, and human experience. Yet its pursuit remains essential. Societies that value truth create stronger relationships, more stable institutions, and more resilient communities. Societies that abandon truth risk losing the foundation upon which cooperation and progress depend.

As you close this book, the journey does not end. It continues in everyday conversations, in decisions about what information to trust, and in the courage to confront uncomfortable realities. The search for truth is not reserved for philosophers, journalists, or scholars. It belongs to anyone willing to remain curious, reflective, and honest — both with others and with themselves.

A society completely free of lies may remain an unreachable ideal. But a society that strives for transparency, responsibility, and thoughtful dialogue is entirely within reach. Every question asked, every fact verified, and every honest conversation becomes a step toward that goal.

The labyrinth will always exist. What matters is how we choose to walk through it — blindly following familiar paths, or consciously searching for the light that leads us forward.

www.ingramcontent.com/pod-product-compliance
Lightning Source LLC
Chambersburg PA
CBHW070206230526
45471CB00002B/849